RETAIL-iation

RETAIL-iation

Serious and Humorous Observations
on Bad Shopping Behavior

DONNA R. SUMMERLIN

iUniverse, Inc.
Bloomington

RETAIL-iation
Serious and Humorous Observations on Bad Shopping Behavior

iUniverse books may be ordered through booksellers or by contacting:

iUniverse
1663 Liberty Drive
Bloomington, IN 47403
www.iuniverse.com
1-800-Authors (1-800-288-4677)

ISBN: 978-1-4620-1280-0 (sc)
ISBN: 978-1-4620-1279-4 (hc)
ISBN: 978-1-4620-1386-9 (ebk)

Library of Congress Control Number: 2011906661

Printed in the United States of America

iUniverse rev. date: 08/01/2011

Contents

Social Shopping Behavior

Retail had never entered my mind as a career choice; many choices had, but never retail. When I graduated from college, I found myself searching for a job in my field of choice; however, after a while, my goal changed. Ultimately I knew what I had to do: get a job—and fast. Strangely enough, just as when a personal relationship you are not searching for happens to you, a relationship with retail happened to me. I enjoyed it, and I was good at it. The world of retail became my world—as far as careers go, anyway. I found it to be rewarding at the end of each and every day; however, as the years went by, I discovered that the relationship was turning into a bad affair. The attraction that bore such a strong foundation had sadly turned into a love-hate relationship. You may find this hard to believe, but, believe it or not, it was not the hard work, the long hours, or even the enormous corporate demands that ultimately brought an end to this long-time affair. It was you—the shopper—that eventually brought it to its closure. Having said that, I believe it's finally time to voice not only my opinions concerning your shopping habits, but also to have a voice for those who still cannot—at least not without the fear of termination. Shoppers, you need to become informed on just how poor—and many times disgusting—your habits are. For the sake of everyone involved in retail, become informed, break your bad habits, and be proud to be a part of making the retail world a better place to shop—not to mention work. It's time to retaliate. It's time for retail-iation.

Face it, all of us are shoppers always shopping for one thing or another—many times for things we don't even need but must have. The truth is, we simply love to shop. So, shopper, why not show some respect for the places where you choose to make your needed purchases? Seriously, what's your problem? We were all taught at very early ages—and teach our kids—to do the right things, starting with the simplest things, such as wiping your feet before entering, putting things back where they came from, cleaning up behind ourselves, saying thank you. Among all the other things, yes, we were all taught to flush. So shoppers, why do these most basic fundamentals of proper manners not apply when you shop? Let it be said to all of you who display common acts of decency, the utmost thanks and respect go out to you because, unfortunately, you are way, way outnumbered.

The Nature of the Beast

Why and when did it become acceptable for you to be so sloppy, lazy, and—most importantly—obnoxiously rude? When did retailers become so vulnerable that they allow your unacceptable behaviors to become the norm? The nature of the beast applies to every career. In retail, the nature of the beast is that TGIF is about as special as TGIM, TGIT, TGIW, and so on. It's just another day. The nature of the beast also means that holidays, unfortunately, are nothing but headaches accompanied by extended hours. These are just a sample of the norms of retail—accept it or get out of it. However, shoppers today have turned into the beast—and it is unnecessary. One by one, you are making an honest effort to save the earth by using green reusable bags instead of plastic ones. I believe that you can—even one by one—change a population of badly behaved shoppers, but it has to start with you.

Your Eyes Are Bigger than Your Budget: Employees End Up Paying for That

For years, I've been waiting to say, "Put it back yourself." Do you realize that—because of your indecisive minds—retailers now have phrases for cleaning up your messes? Go-backs and put-backs are just part of the list. I say, "Put it back yourself." Who are you to decide the extra jobs of others? No, cleaning up your mess doesn't necessarily fall within anyone's job description—you simply add this hectic task to an already hectic day. I just don't get it. You pick up items—yet when you are checking out—you simply decide that you don't want certain ones. You think nothing of saying, "I don't want these." I want to say to you, "I don't want them either." I just don't get it. Some of you have discovered interesting ways to be assured that your child will behave while you shop. Anything and everything your child may want goes right into the cart, knowing full well that you have no intentions of purchasing them. Without any regard to the store's personnel—and, more importantly, to your child—you leave all of these items at the checkout register. I say, "Shame on you." That is most certainly a pathetic path you have taken to discipline your child.

Most of the time, you don't even wait until you reach the checkout register to display your inability to decide what you want and do not want. Most of the time, you—without

4

thinking anything about it—go through the store and begin remerchandising it, leaving all types of items that you have chosen in all kinds of places—obviously where they do not belong. One word says it all: *lazy*. You have no regard for the value of an item if you've decided you no longer want it or can afford it. In many cases, you create an astounding amount of waste. I'm here to inform you that frozen and cold foods are just that—frozen or cold—and should remain that way while in a store. If you choose to toss them in your medicine cabinet when you get home, by all means, do so. Otherwise, in a store, leave them be if your eyes are bigger than your budget. Add it up, folks—you all do it. Add up the costs, which, by the way, ultimately fall directly back on you. Whether it is a landfill of go-backs that can go back, or those that must be written-off, the loss due to extra payroll and waste will always end up coming out of your pocket in the end. So if you don't want it, resist it. If you can't resist—but find that you can't purchase it—put it back where you got it. Stop being so lazy—it's not that hard. My suggestion is if you know you shop with your eyes rather than your budget, then make a list and train yourself to not just check it twice, but to stick to it. Stop being a shopping slob and, one by one, a difference can be made. That difference can start with you.

Out of Order

B an them! Ban all restrooms from the public—at least until members of the public learn to clean up their act. That's all I have to say about that. After all, it is a crappy subject.

Cash Management 101

I've never had a card thrown at me or randomly tossed all over the counter. Cash, however, is a completely different ballgame. You toss your crumbled bills—and your many pennies, nickels, dimes, and quarters—all over the place. It makes no sense. You don't like to wait, but your bad action causes a wait—not just for you, but for those behind you. The funny thing is that they have a tendency to do the exact same thing. What is it? What thrill do you achieve? Clearly, there is someone there with an available hand to receive your payment. It is degrading to have to pick up your pennies, nickels, and dimes. It is degrading to unfold your bills. I just don't get it. Do you want your change returned to you in that fashion? It can be done, but someone would lose his or her job. It would please no one more than the person behind the counter that you so degraded to treat you with that fashion of payment. I guarantee you that you would demand his or her termination. Terminate yourself first. No one likes to be treated with such disrespect. I believe that many of you don't even give it a thought; however, you would if it happened to you. Those of you who are control freaks, well, you are understood—not forgiven, but understood. Note that this is not a good thing. Those of you who are germaphobes, well, it's too late—everything has been touched already, including the money you're about to so rudely toss. I know that we will eventually become a cashless society. I also know that it will not be soon enough.

Blinded by the Light

Wow! Who knew that register lights serve a purpose? In most places, the days of people leaning on their register, cleaning out their fingernails while smacking on a piece of Juicy Fruit gum are long over. Multitasking is the name of the game. Companies get more bang for their buck with one person doing the job of two—and many times three or more. Simply said, that is how it is. So, stop with the "duh, where do I check out?" look and go to a register with a light on. One of the most ridiculous questions I've ever heard is "Is there someone to check me out?" So many times I've wanted to say, "No not today—we're too busy." Seriously, what do you think? The registers have lights so that you know where to check out—regardless of whether someone is waiting there. The registers are being watched by those assigned to them in addition to their other tasks.

Multitasking is becoming more popular; the concept has proven to be successful without sacrificing the top priority: quality customer service. This may not be true for all, but I will stick my neck out and say that I do believe it is true for most. Also, there is no need to yell, "Hello" or bang on the register. It's especially funny, however, when you're not even at one that is running. We get a good—maybe cheap—laugh out of that. You make fools of yourselves when you do things of this nature. You simply need to understand that—in between customers—everyone is required to be productive in other ways. Quality customer service is the top priority and can be achieved while simultaneously achieving other tasks that ultimately benefit you, the shopper. So stop making fools of yourselves—dive right in, take a chance, risk it all, and simply go to the damn light. It works like magic.

Blinded by the Light?
You Can Find a Line in the Dark

A h, the dreaded line. You know where to check out, but what do you do? You bitch about it. Drive-through lines, traffic lines, theater lines, and of course, the most dreaded of all—lines on your face—all occur. How many long traffic lights have you sat through only to sit longer because of those in front of you? Lines occur every day. They occur everywhere. Accept it—and get over it. You don't abandon your vehicle if you get stuck in a long line of traffic, but you most definitely will abandon your shopping cart if the mood strikes. If you choose to continue in the line, you grunt, you huff and puff, you do everything but blow the house down. Take a pill—lines happen. They happen for so many reasons and, believe it or not, the retailer dislikes them much more than you do.

Lines occur for too many reasons to count, and, no, they are not pleasant to be in—unless you get to know your neighbor. People do call out for their shift for various reasons: they have to (per OSHA) take their well-deserved breaks, technology sometimes fails, and many times you're not ready with your payment. You know you have to pay for your purchase and have waited in line, but you wait until the last minute to realize that your money is in the car. So many times you—the shopper, the one complaining about waiting—create an even longer line by simply not being ready. However, it's okay then because it's all about you. In a perfect world, there would always be people on the bench to back up any shortages of help whenever needed. In the real world, however, that doesn't happen. There is no payroll budget big enough to accommodate a second string of players to get into the game.

I want to take this opportunity to personally thank someone I don't even know—and, sadly, she will probably never know it. I can't even remember if it was a Christmas Eve or a rare snowy morning, but I was in the store by myself because of an unusual circumstance: call-outs. As manager, you have to drop everything and do what first and foremost has to be done. You open up and tend to your customers at checkout; you cannot afford to be anywhere else or do anything else. My line grew—and continued to grow—no matter how good or fast I was. In keeping with courteous customer service, I was working as swiftly as possible to keep the line moving. Someone happened to overhear me say that I hadn't even had my coffee. No more than fifteen minutes had passed before a cup of McDonald's coffee was handed to me. Someone said, "Heard you hadn't had your coffee." This was many years ago, but it hasn't been forgotten. To this day, that still remains one of the best cups of coffee I've ever had—not because of where it came from, but from the kindness it stemmed from. No one likes to wait in a line, but because many times they are inevitable, show some restraint, accept it, and move on. There are worse things.

The Gender Gap in Shopping

Yes, there actually is a noticeable difference in the way men and women shop. Males, without a doubt, make better shoppers. If there is not a list in their hand, there's at least one in their head. They still possess the common tendency to buy on impulse while shopping. If they pick it up, it's in the bag. Ladies, you could learn a thing or two by observing their technique. They tend to be direct, meticulous, and definitely methodic. Women, on the other hand, don't seem to possess quite the same amount of finesse. List or no list, women always seem to be questioning their choice of purchases. I guess that's where a woman's prerogative comes into play. Guys, you get the thumbs-up from me for shopping with a sense of style.

Can You Hear Me Now?

You ask, "Can you hear me?" How can I when you're busy yapping away on your cell at check-out? Rude, rude, rude, rude, and more rude. Just in case you don't know by now, allow me—it's rude. You should only shop in stores that provide self check-outs. I've often had the urge to pick up the register phone, or even better yet, pull out my cell and make a casual, random call while checking you out, but I could never allow myself to stoop to such a low level—you know, your level.

Wow. . . Free Day Care

First and foremost, we are not your babysitters. Our job description includes many tasks and requires many talents, but child care is most definitely not one of them. Seriously, you drop your kids off and then proceed to shop in other places that your kids might not be so enthusiastic about. If they run wild and you're not around, we suddenly become guardians.

There are times that you have to pick them up from school because of illness—whether it is chicken pox, strep throat, or head lice. What do you do? You bring them with you to do your shopping. It makes no sense—at least not to me. The reasons are quite obvious why they have been sent home from school. It may sound cruel, but retailers should be able to do the very same thing. Take them home—that's where they belong. By the way, when you're sick, you also need to stay home and stop spreading your nasty germs all over the place.

As for healthy kids, they run around opening toys and playing with them while you're around. The funny thing is, you don't feel as if you should pay for them because you didn't tell them that they could have them. Your kid just made a sellable product unsellable, yet you don't think that you should have to pay for it—ridiculous. This brings to mind a phrase that has stuck with me throughout the years: bad action. I heard this phrase from a customer and use it sometimes to this day, but usually in a sarcastic fashion. This woman's kid was a tyrant who tore up everything within sight and reach. In her modern-day method of parenting, she said, "Bad action." By the time I was finished tallying up the losses incurred, she really didn't care for her bad-action bill.

We shouldn't have to be the ones stopping your kids from running throughout the store, throwing footballs down the aisles, kicking balls, spraying crazy string everywhere, and the list goes on. All in all, these kids belong to you—not the store. Stop expecting us to raise them.

Sorry, We're Closed

What an awful thing to hear and endure. Some of you would rather hear that your spouse has just died. You act as if it's the end of the world, many times leaving us feeling as if condolences are in order. My advice is this: quit tucking your tail between your legs, hanging your head down, and begging to get in. It is not a pretty picture. Simply go to an at-your-beck-and-call store—you know, the one that is open twenty-four hours and never closes. Yes, you will most likely pay more, but if you really need something, then it's worth the price. After all, you are paying them to be at your beck and call.

I want to share a special closing moment that has remained unforgettable for me. Our posted hours let customers know we were open at 9:00 a.m. and closed at 9:00 p.m. It seems simple, but, unfortunately, it is not for some. I was in my office at eight in the morning. I could hear someone repeatedly knocking on the doors, which obviously were locked. Since he was a regular customer, I unlocked the door and opened it slightly. I said, "We don't open until nine."

He kept staring at the posted hours but appeared somewhat irritated and confused.

I repeated, "We don't open until nine."

He responded, "So you're closing early?"

Well, bless his soul, as well as mine—I was the one that had to inform him that it was eight in the morning and not eight at night.

Memorable Moments: Where's Amnesia When You Need It?

Your gum has lost its flavor. Oh my—so tragic. It has to go. Go ahead, spit it on the floor—everyone else does.

"Crap, I forgot my chew spit can." Well, don't worry—there's a shelf right there.

Your child's diaper is messy? Not a problem—just stash it inside the nearest floor display. It always sucks to be the lucky one to find it.

Feel the sudden urge for a douche? Steal one and use it in the store you stole it from—real sad for many reasons.

Craving some Vienna sausages? Paid for or not, please, eat them all. Leaving a half-eaten Vienna sausage on the shelf could actually lead to your arrest for theft. Please, cover your tracks—don't leave the evidence.

Gotta throw up? Grab the nearest bucket, but, no, don't bother to purchase it.

"I just left the doctor's office; he said I have the swine flu." Well, thanks for coming in.

What's up with toothpicks? Is it written that it's proper to toss them anywhere when you no longer need to pick your teeth? Same goes for snotty tissues. Speaking of teeth and tissues, I must say, this person remains blameless. We found someone's teeth wrapped in tissue. Funny—no one ever claimed those teeth.

Purchase a curved, beveled-glass frame, drop it as you approach your car, then go back into the store with your frame in many pieces and say, "I don't know if this was like this when I got it."

When a bathroom is out of order, stop making it more out of order than it already is.

Not sure whether what you're looking for is the right size, color, whatever? Go ahead—open it up. Yes, it's exactly what you need. Purchase the one you opened? What? That's unheard of.

Handicap parking spaces are designated for cars, not carts no matter their condition.

The Oscar for Best Dramatic Performance

Although the abundance of talent out there is radically astounding, my vote for best performance goes to a group that rises above all the others in creating unforgettable, award-winning moments. And the Oscar goes to . . . the "I-gave-you-a-twenty" group. With performances so seemingly authentic, so well-crafted, and, most importantly, so well-timed, even a seasoned pro such as myself has fallen for them an embarrassingly countless amount of times, resulting in tills not so popular in the box-office. In terms of cash-handling—even when the error of margin is calculated in—I dare say that 99.9 percent of the time, no twenty is ever a true role player. You're the player. Yes, many times I do believe that the act is quite genuine, that it is honest, and you believe it to be true. However, you crafty little souls should truly be on the red carpet—or at least have your own star on the boulevard. To some of you, on the other hand, I say, "Keep your day job." If there's no line at the check-out register, it's simple to stop and do a cash-drawer audit to solve the twenty-dollar-bill mystery without interrupting the flow of business, hence downplaying your dramatic performance. My personal favorite, "I gave you a twenty," has become a register sitcom classic: "Geez, it's a brand new till—I have no twenties." Even though you don't make the cut, the look on your face is not only awesome, it's award-winning.

The Runner-Up Performance

There are actors—and then there are the overreactors. For instance, you might be able to pull rabbits out of your hat, but I can't pull rabbits or plush dogs out of mine. A rather interesting character had shopped with us for years; her behavior oftentimes seemed like a child—and many times was downright neurotic. One of those times deserves an honorable mention. I admit today—as I did then—that she was somewhat inconvenienced, though innocently. Having been mistakenly told in a phone call from another affiliated store that we had plush dogs in stock, she traveled to our location. When she arrived, she discovered that the plush dogs had sold out. Apologies were running rampant. Well, for her, there could never be enough apologies. Since I wasn't a magician and I didn't wear hats, I could not magically pull these plush dogs out of one. In reality, all we could do was to apologize for her inconvenience and the fifteen minutes of wasted time and gas. Ballistic would mildly describe what seemed to be her never-ending scene. This inconvenience cost no lives—nor did I allow it to cost anyone his or her job. I believe that she was a preschool teacher. It's sad to say that she's learning more from them than they are from her. She has the temper-tantrum act down pat.

BYOB

No, no, no, not bring your own bottle—that was yesterday. Today, it means bring your own bag. It's a great concept—helping with the effort to save the planet and helping corporations make more money and save more money by marketing green ones and cutting their costs on the purchase of disposable ones. I will say it is a much-needed trend—and I hope that it only grows in popularity. However, I wish that the reusable bag could be somewhat more user-friendly—for employees, anyway.

Since most checkouts are designed for the not-so-popular plastic bag, the bagging process loses its flow. Companies should take their savings and redesign the registers to coincide with today's shopping trends. Now, let's do a little bag talk. Since you're so proud to be a part of this effort to save the earth, for everyone's sake, remember that you're attempting to do so. Why wait until your purchases are bagged to say, "Oh, I brought my own bags" and expect them to be rebagged? If you want to join the no-plastic revolution, why make the green bags—that you are so proudly purchasing—the last items on the checkout belt, leaving everything that has already been bagged to be bagged again?

There are also those of you who, despite the best intentions, fail to say that you don't need a bag—after your items are bagged. You expect your items to be removed from the bag? I say, "Remove them yourself." Be responsible when you BYOB.

A Thing of the Past

U nfortunately, those wonderful corner stores have become a thing of the past. Seeing their remnants on highways may take you back to the good times, but, for the most part, corner stores have become extinct. What an outright shame. Corporate America has taken over, and we have all allowed it to happen, putting the small-town shops out of business. Back in the days of true general stores, people were polite and kids were well-behaved. John-Boy would have had his John-butt put in its place if he had behaved in Godsey's Store the way kids do today. For those of you who are clueless at this point, check out the classic *Waltons* series. I have noticed that the stores that try to integrate the old with the new—which I choose to shop in—have shoppers that are more pleasant, creating a pleasant shopping experience. The lack of hostility that is felt in other stores is noticeable. How unfortunate it is that today's generation knows these stores as the not-so-conveniently-priced, but friendly, convenience store.

More Memorable Moments

"Why don't you take your fat ass home and let somebody else check me out?"

Well, that's a hell of a thing to say to someone who obviously is in training. Everyone has to learn and, to me, doing is learning. This was actually said to a new associate in training—pleasant indeed. I want to know what difference the size of someone's ass really makes as far as whether they know what they're doing? I will speak for her when I say, "Take your own ass home."

"I'm not your sweetie."

I know with all of today's sexual harassment issues, laws, and concerns, words such as *sweetie*, *honey*, *baby*, and *love* are considered inappropriate. However, I also know that we can all distinguish between innocence and malicious intent. I also know that the laws exist so that there is no line to draw. Once again, however, you should be able to recognize the difference between someone's innocence and kindness versus any unruly intent.

"I'm not your" sweetie" was said to a truly honest and hard working co-worker of mine. She was raised to be a sweet Southern girl, but I knew that she would eventually be whipped by the lash of someone's tongue. I saw it on her face; her beautiful, young spirit had been broken. I know the only thing necessary to say would have been, "Hey, how are you doing? Did you find everything you needed?" I can't hold back and bite my tongue at this point. I want to say, on her behalf, "Hey, bitch, how ya' doin'?" Be careful where you travel to. Sometimes you might just find yourself in nice, friendly places. Respect them when you do because, in this day and time, consider yourself fortunate.

"Do you work here?"

"No, I found this shirt and nametag on the street, and I really liked them."

"Where have you moved the Doritos to now?"

"Look underneath your elbow—you're leaning on the stack-out display."

Priceless.

Where's a Referee When You Need One?

" Customers are always right—even when they're wrong."
What? It just might be best if I simply walk away and
leave that one alone.

No, no, no—I can't do it. I must say, and please note that it
is from the bottom of my heart, "My butt."

Call Someone Who Cares

S hoppers are fortunate to have someone to complain to and, yes, they should, because there are times when associates act inappropriately. Those actions need to be addressed and nipped in the bud as soon as possible. Almost every company has a number to call if your complaint can't be—or isn't—handled in the field, otherwise known as the store level. With every right, you call someone who cares, otherwise known as the corporate office.

Who do *we* call when you behave inappropriately? Who do *we* call when you are abusive and offensive? There isn't anyone, and you know it. You behave in any fashion you so desire, and it's considered acceptable because, to you, that's a part of our job. In reality, seriously, how many times in your life have you been treated inappropriately? The playing field is not quite fair. We are way outnumbered and are abused on a daily basis. No, we have no one to call because, frankly, no one cares.

A Life Sentence

Yes, we have done it to ourselves, leaving no one but ourselves to blame for this life sentence—a life imprisoned by the walls of the retail world. It's sad to say, but many times it feels like an abusive relationship you've become so accustomed to that you're more afraid to leave than to stay. You find more fear in the unknown than you do in driving to work every day. For some reason, you feel secure because you feel it's all you know, while sadly, sacrificing your dignity and your self-esteem. I know I'm not speaking for all, however. I also know that I'm speaking for many and it's a real shame because the retail world is actually a fascinating place to be and work. Sometimes it's as if I have traveled the world two times over because of the many cultures I have been fortunate enough to meet and sometimes know.

It's an ever-changing place because of ever-changing products and activities. I find it to be a hard-working, stressful, but—most importantly—fascinating place of work. However, the downfall that coincides with this fascination breaks bones that cannot be medically repaired. Over time, it breaks your spirit and your soul. As a mom or dad, you can put a smile back on your child's face with a simple Band-Aid on a skinned knee. However, it's not so easy to heal a broken spirit.

For young people, learning the mental ropes of retail is a hard rope to tug. Many times, they just want to quit and run away. Many times I wanted to tell them to run—and run just as fast as they could. Instead, I resorted to what got me through my days over and over again. I always fell back on one thing—and most of the times I could see the nerves calming down and the tears drying up.

I said, "How many people have you waited on today?"

They would say, "I don't know—a lot."

I said, "Then don't let this one person do this to you. They're probably like that everywhere they go, making everyone around them just as miserable as they have made you. Shake it off and move on."

Over time, I decided that it was time for me to move on to the finish line and find the victory of relief. It was time for a change. It was time to stop trying to play the role of a retail psychologist and not allow this somewhat voluntarily chosen life sentence to turn into a walk on death row. Life is way too short, and I knew I needed to start running for mine.

The Finish Line

It's a hard line to draw, define, or to believe in, but I imagined the line, put a definition to it, and—after some time—believed in it. I knew that it was time for me to cross one finish line and start running a different race. Fear of change shadowed me, placing the finish line farther and farther away. My drive to cross that line finally overcame the fear of change. I have felt the thrill of victory many times in my life, but, I have to say that this run—this finish—has proven to be my personal best. One knows when it's time for a refreshing change—and I knew it was my time. The long-time relationship that I lived for, longed for, and believed in had lost its zest—and everyone needs zest. The bottom line is that—no matter how long my relationship with retail, no matter how many good times we had together—I knew I was no longer happy. I was not the least bit satisfied or content. I threw caution into the wind and set sail in search of the me that, for many years, was simply—and sadly—just existing.

For all of you in retail—and for all of you who shop—I have written this book with the hope that poor shopping behavior will improve. Change is contagious. If this book can wake one person up about his or her awareness when it comes to the fundamentals of good manners, then it has served its purpose.

For all of you in retail, my hat is off to you and my glass is held high. So many of us share a common bond—a common thread—that somehow ties us together in a way that we can only begin to understand.

Express Yourself Here With Your Own Personal Favorites

....

....

....

....

....

....

....

....

....

....

....

....

....

....

....

....

....

....

Express Yourself

....
....
....
....
....
....
....
....
....
....
....
....
....
....
....
....
....

Express Yourself

....
....
....
....
....
....
....
....
....
....
....
....
....
....
....
....
....
....

Express Yourself

Express Yourself

....
....
....
....
....
....
....
....
....
....
....
....
....
....
....
....
....
....
....

Express Yourself

....

....

....

....

....

....

....

....

....

....

....

....

....

....

....

....

....

Express Yourself

....
....
....
....
....
....
....
....
....
....
....
....
....
....
....
....
....
....

Express Yourself

Express Yourself

....

....

....

....

....

....

....

....

....

....

....

....

....

....

....

....

....

....

Express Yourself

Express Yourself

....
....
....
....
....
....
....
....
....
....
....
....
....
....
....
....
....
....

Express Yourself

....
....
....
....
....
....
....
....
....
....
....
....
....
....
....
....
....
....

Express Yourself

....

....

....

....

....

....

....

....

....

....

....

....

....

....

....

....

....

....

www.ingramcontent.com/pod-product-compliance
Lightning Source LLC
Chambersburg PA
CBHW051252170526
45165CB00004B/1676